THE OFFICIAL
ABERDEEN
ANNUAL 2009

A Grange Publication

Written by Malcolm Panton

Designed by Colin Heggie

© 2008. Published by Grange Communications Ltd., Edinburgh,
under licence from Aberdeen Football Club.
Printed in the EU.

Every effort has been made to ensure the accuracy of information within this publication but the
publishers cannot be held responsible for any errors or omissions. Views expressed are those of the
author and do not necessarily represent those of the publishers or the football club.
All rights reserved.

Photography by Newsline Scotland, Kara Griffiths

ISBN 978-1-906211-62-2

£6.99

CONTENTS 2009

MEET THE MANAGER

FOUR SEASONS AT PITTODRIE, FOUR TOP SIX FINISHES – YOU CAN'T COMPLAIN ABOUT JIMMY CALDERWOOD'S CONSISTENCY CAN YOU!?

Since joining the Dons from Dunfermline back in 2004, after spells coaching in Holland, Jimmy has put Aberdeen firmly back at the top of the Scottish game, making us one of the most feared sides outwith the Old Firm and their multi-millions.

Jimmy was also responsible for taking the club back into Europe and last season's UEFA Cup campaign is one that we will all remember for a very long time, especially if you were at Pittodrie on the nights we played Copenhagen and Bayern Munich.

The next task on Jimmy's agenda is to take the club to Hampden and some cup finals, because it's too long since the Dons were in one of those. We came agonisingly close last term, losing at the semi-final stage in the Scottish Cup and the CIS, but who's to say we can't go a step further this time around?

If we don't, it won't be for a lack of effort. Jimmy Calderwood will make sure of that!

YOUR CITY YOUR TEAM

YOU'LL HAVE ALL SEEN THE AFC TV ADVERT BY NOW, BUT NOBODY HAS SEEN BEHIND THE SCENES YET!

THESE ARE THE STARS OF THE SHOW BEING PUT THROUGH THEIR PACES BY THE CAMERA CREW AND DIRECTOR – CAN YOU BELIEVE BRAD PITT TURNED US DOWN?!?

SEASON REVIEW

A SEASON THAT PROMISED MUCH, DELIVERED FAR MORE THAN WE COULD HAVE EXPECTED BUT WHICH FINALLY DISAPPOINTED AT HAMPDEN. IT WAS SOME SEASON...

JULY / AUGUST

The summer saw skipper Russell Anderson leave for Sunderland, Scott Severin taking on the armband in his place. Coming in to Pittodrie were Jeffrey de Visscher, Lee Mair, Jackie McNamara and the surprise return of Derek Young.

It was a case of "Carry On Up The Nile" as the squad headed for Egypt for its pre-season training camp before returning for four tough SPL games in August. Late defeat at Tannadice set the tone for a season of "so near but so far" at league level, a theme repeated throughout the month. Hearts grabbed an equaliser in first half injury time to draw 1-1 at Pittodrie and after leading Celtic for much of the next game, two goals in the last five minutes gave the Bhoys a 3-1 win.

Having dominated much of the next game at Easter Road, the Dons had a 3-1 lead going into the final 20 minutes but still contrived to come away with just a 3-3 draw. Craig Brewster had been in great form for us up front, but he ended the month by returning to Inverness Caley Thistle to take over as manager.

SEPTEMBER

A first SPL win of the season came with a 1-0 win at Kilmarnock but that was quickly countered when Motherwell showed they would be a force under Mark McGhee by winning 2-1 at Pittodrie.

September was all about Europe and the visit of Dnipro in the UEFA Cup, the qualifying game ahead of the group stage. The Ukrainians were tough but the Dons gave us another taster for the season ahead, saving their best for Europe, fighting out a very useful 0-0 draw to take to eastern Europe.

Playing Rangers on the Sunday was too tough, the Gers winning 3-0, but we made progress in the CIS by beating Partick 2-0, Derek Young and "Cup-Tie" Considine both on the scoresheet. Rounding the month off by beating Gretna with some ease, 2-0, the season was beginning to gather momentum.

OCTOBER

And then it went ballistic as Darren Mackie threw himself at a Richard Foster's cross to head into the Dnipro net. A terrific, backs to the wall defensive performance followed and though Dnipro grabbed an equaliser with 15 minutes to go, Aberdeen saw it through to grab a place in the group stage of the UEFA Cup for the first time.

A thumping 4-0 win over St Mirren — two goals apiece for Severin and Lee Miller — and then a 2-1 triumph over Inverness and the Dons were back in the top six of the SPL and the garden was looking rosy. A 3-0 defeat out in Greece at the hands of Panathinaikos reminded us that we still had a lot of learning to do on the European stage, but the prospect of three more games to come held plenty of promise.

The same was true of the CIS, the Dons marching into the semi-final courtesy of a 4-1 blitzing of Inverness Caley Thistle, Barry Nicholson's hat-trick proving to be decisive. In the end, the draw paired us with Dundee United, though not before it had descended into chaos at Holyrood with the wrong teams being paired and for a few hours, we thought we were playing Rangers. Might have been better to have left it like that as it turned out.

NOVEMBER

A 2-0 win over our upcoming semi-final opponents put us in 5th and in good nick for the visit of Lokomotiv Moscow. Zander gave us an early lead and all went well until the Russian outfit nicked an equaliser on the brink of half-time, an all too familiar story.

Coming back to the SPL on the Sunday proved tough again and we ended up beaten 4-1 at Hearts, then losing 3-0 at Parkhead to drop out of the top half of the table ahead of the trek to Atletico Madrid. The Dons gave a good account of themselves against an undeniably impressive team. Once again, the seconds before half-time were crucial, Atletico going ahead with a penalty, then fortune favoured them with a free-kick on the hour mark – they were lucky to get it, then lucky to see it go in after it rebounded off the post and in off Jamie Langfield. Now we had to see if results elsewhere would render the Copenhagen game meaningless or not.

DECEMBER

With perhaps just one UEFA game left, we got down to the business of trying to qualify again by reeling off back to back SPL wins at the start of December, though another reverse at the hands of Motherwell did little for the cause.

By then though, all eyes were on the upcoming game with Copenhagen. A win and the Dons were in the knock-out stages, easier said than done against a Danish team bristling with Champions League experience. Goalless at half-time, the Dons suddenly exploded after the break and tore their much fancied opponents to pieces.

Jamie Smith started the rout with two crackers before the hour mark and when Antonsson diverted a Miller cross into his own net after 71 minutes, Pittodrie was going berserk. When Foster made it 4-0 after 83 minutes, the icing was duly applied to the cake and the Dons had completed an immense achievement, a tale only made better by the fact that we came out of the hat alongside Bayern Munich for the next round.

Post-Europe challenges don't come any tougher than Rangers but we slugged out a draw with the Gers, Miller equalising the opener from Adam after McCulloch got sent off. Boxing Day was disappointing with only a draw at Gretna, Steve Lovell coming off the bench to score after 86 minutes only for Gretna to equalise in the last minute – told you it was a recurring theme. Even so, a 1-0 win in Paisley saw us climb to fifth in the SPL once more, six points behind third placed Motherwell.

JANUARY

It's always good to start the new year well and a 1-0 win over Inverness Caley Thistle and a 0-0 draw at Falkirk saw us move up to fourth and closer to Motherwell, inactive following the tragic death of Phil O'Donnell.

Falkirk were the opponents again in a more exciting Scottish Cup, the Dons twice taking the lead in the first ten minutes before getting pegged back in the second half and forced into a replay – another game we didn't need given the heavy fixture schedule. A grim 3-0 beating at Tannadice followed, though victory in the

Falkirk replay did lift the spirits as Aberdeen continued in fine cup form, big game Jamie Smith striking twice, another goal coming from de Visscher in the 3-1 triumph.

January saw the end of two long Pittodrie careers with Chris Clark and Michael Hart both following Russell Anderson down south while Stuart Duff and Alan Maybury joined the Dons. The month ended on a low, defeat at home to Hearts making a UEFA Cup place look decidedly dodgy, putting greater emphasis on the upcoming Scottish Cup fourth round.

FEBRUARY

Not that we knew who we were playing. After a Monday night replay, it seemed we would be playing Brechin. Then Hamilton appealed against the result on the grounds that Brechin had fielded ineligible players. Our game was off as a replay between the two was on the cards until, at 11.30 on Thursday morning, Brechin were thrown out of the cup and Hamilton reinstated. In the end, the Dons sneaked through to the next round 1-0.

And so to the CIS Insurance Cup semi-final, and a meeting with Dundee United. It all started so well, Considine scoring another cup goal to set us on our way, Dods equalising quickly afterwards. It was the second half when the roof fell in though, Langfield showered with missiles from the United end, United then scoring twice in five minutes just after the hour before sealing victory with a fourth goal on 77 minutes. Not the best preparation for a visit from Celtic. Ironically, the Dons played far better than the scoreline suggested, but nonetheless, a 5-1 drubbing saw Aberdeen's league campaign coming swiftly off the rails.

Nine goals shipped in two games and Bayern Munich with Toni, Podolski and Klose our next visitors. But the Dons discovered their best European form in front of the Germans and in front of Europe's TV cameras. Sone Aluko and Josh Walker both scored cracking goals as the Dons shared four goals with Bayern in an epic performance, a game that with a shade more fortune, we might well have won. The Dons took that form to Easter Road, played Hibs off the park for long stretches of the game and promptly lost 3-1 to drop to 8th in the SPL.

The following week saw the trip to Munich and the awesome stadium and facilities that Germany's footballing aristocracy can boast. We also saw something of their awesome talent as Bayern turned on the style. The final scoreline of 5-1 might have flattered the Bundesliga team a little but there's no denying their quality.

The month was rounded out with a 3-1 defeat at Kilmarnock and then a 1-1 draw against Motherwell, underlining that the season now came down to one competition, the Scottish Cup, the only realistic route to a place in Europe.

MARCH

Defeat at Ibrox took us down to 8th in the SPL, reinforcing the need to beat Celtic in the following week's quarter-final, the more so since the draw was made before the game, giving the winners the incentive of a semi-final tie with Queen of the South. It looked as though Aberdeen were set fair to go through, leading through a de Visscher goal 11 minutes from time but fellow Dutchman Vennegoor of Hesselink dragged Celtic level with virtually the last kick of the game. Chance gone, surely?

We had another week where we didn't know if Saturday's game would go ahead but finally, Gretna were allowed to stumble on, the Dons coming through to win 3-0. And so to Celtic Park where Mackie repeated his Dnipro magic, scoring his second goal of the season to win another tie nobody believed we had a prayer of coming through. A second semi-final of the

season awaited us, against a First Division side. Surely no mistakes this time?

A draw at home to St Mirren made a top six place look unlikely but in a dramatic game, Chris Maguire poached a late winner to win the game 4-3 at Inverness Caley Thistle. We clung to faint hopes.

APRIL

Results elsewhere conspired to ensure that a win over Falkirk would see us into the top six for a fourth consecutive season and Maguire provided that winner with just eight minutes to go. More escapes than David Blaine!

The luck ran out at Hampden the following Saturday though. Starting poorly against Queen of the South, we were a goal down before Cup-tie Considine struck to get us level going into

half-time. From there, the Dons would click into gear and win the game wouldn't they?

There followed what must be the most bizarre 11 minutes of any Scottish Cup semi-final ever as five goals flew, Queen's scoring, the Dons instantly responding until, on the hour, John Stewart made it 4-3 and we found we had run out of equalisers. A certain place in Europe gone and a chance of winning another trophy gone with it. A grim day.

A trip to Parkhead followed and some pride was restored as we lost 1-0 courtesy of a Samaras strike and a howler from Iain Brines who admitted later that he had disallowed a perfectly good late equaliser from Diamond. Not really been our year for luck, has it? It looked that way against Hibs too as the Dons dominated but went a goal behind before coming back to win the game 2-1 as two Hibs men saw red, Aberdeen keeping those slender hopes of a third place finish just about alive.

MAY

And so the never ending season went on, and hope sprang eternal after a tough battle with Dundee United at Pittodrie saw the Dons come through, 2-1, and narrow the gap to third place to just three points. Did we dare to dream? Well, if Richard Foster and Karim Touzani were going to start scoring goals, anything was possible.

Of course, if referees and their assistants were going to ignore perfectly good goals – as they did with Nicholson's effort that crossed the line when it stood 1-1 at Motherwell – there was no hope. Had that stood we might well have won the game but losing our second good goal in four games was pivotal and Motherwell went on to claim victory.

The final game was Rangers, the Dons running out 2-0 winners to deny Rangers the title and earn ourselves fourth place in the SPL. Not a bad finish after all!

2007/08 RESULTS

DATE	OPPONENTS	RESULT	SCORERS
Sat 4 Aug	Dundee United	0-1	
Sun 12 Aug	HEARTS	1-1	Nicholson
Sun 19 Aug	CELTIC	1-3	Brewster
Sat 25 Aug	Hibernian	3-3	Brewster 2, J Smith
Sat 1 Sep	Kilmarnock	1-0	Miller
Sat 15 Sep	MOTHERWELL	1-2	J Smith
Thu 20 Sep	Dnipro (UEFA 1 1st leg)	0-0	
Sun 23 Sep	Rangers	0-3	
Wed 26 Sep	Partick Thistle (CIS3)	2-0	Young, Considine
Sat 29 Sep	GRETNA	2-0	Diamond, J Smith
Thu 4 Oct	Dnipro (UEFA 1 2nd leg)	1-1	Mackie
Sun 7 Oct	ST MIRREN	4-0	Severin 2, Miller 2
Sun 21 Oct	Inverness Caley Thistle	2-1	Young, Tokely (og)
Thu 25 Oct	Panathinaikos (UEFA Group)	0-3	
Sun 28 Oct	FALKIRK	1-1	Severin
Wed 31 Oct	Inverness Caley Thistle (CIS4)	4-1	Nicholson 3, Miller
Sat 3 Nov	DUNDEE UNITED	2-0	Aluko, Miller
Thu 8 Nov	LOKO MOSCOW (UEFA Group)	1-1	Diamond
Sun 11 Nov	Hearts	1-4	de Visscher
Sat 24 Nov	Celtic	0-3	
Thu 29 Nov	Atletico Madrid (UEFA Group)	0-2	
Sun 2 Dec	HIBERNIAN	3-1	Miller, Clark, Young
Sat 8 Dec	KILMARNOCK	2-1	Nicholson, Miller
Sat 15 Dec	Motherwell	0-3	
Thu 20 Dec	COPENHAGEN (UEFA Group)	4-0	J Smith 2, Antonsson (og), Foster
Sun 23 Dec	RANGERS	1-1	Miller
Wed 26 Dec	Gretna	1-1	Lovell
Sat 29 Dec	St Mirren	1-0	Lovell
Wed 2 Jan	Inverness Caley Thistle	1-0	Nicholson
Sat 5 Jan	Falkirk	0-0	
Sat 12 Jan	Falkirk (SC4)	2-2	J Smith, Lovell
Sat 19 Jan	Dundee United	0-3	
Tue 22 Jan	FALKIRK (SC4 R)	3-1	J Smith 2, de Visscher
Sat 26 Jan	HEARTS	0-1	
Sat 2 Feb	HAMILTON (SC5)	1-0	Diamond
Tue 5 Feb	Dundee United (CIS SF)	1-4	Considine
Sun 10 Feb	CELTIC	1-5	Miller
Thu 14 Feb	BAYERN MUNICH (UEFA1st leg)	2-2	Walker, Aluko
Sun 17 Feb	Hibernian	1-3	Diamond
Thu 21 Feb	Bayern Munich (UEFA 2nd leg)	1-5	Lovell
Sun 24 Feb	Kilmarnock	1-3	Combe (og)
Wed 27 Feb	MOTHERWELL	1-1	Diamond
Sat 1 Mar	Rangers	1-3	Lovell
Sun 9 Mar	CELTIC (SC6)	1-1	de Visscher
Tue 15 Mar	GRETNA	3-0	Maguire, Miller, Nicholson
Tue 18 Mar	Celtic (SC6R)	1-0	Mackie
Sat 22 Mar	ST MIRREN	1-1	Mair
Sat 29 Mar	Inverness Caley Thistle	4-3	Aluko, Nicholson, Miller, Maguire
Mon 7 Apr	FALKIRK	2-1	Maguire 2
Sat 12 Apr	Queen of the South (SC SF)	3-4	Considine 2, Nicholson
Sat 19 Apr	Celtic	0-1	
Sat 26 Apr	HIBERNIAN	2-1	Mackie, Miller
Sat 3 May	DUNDEE UNITED	2-1	Foster, Touzani
Sat 10 May	Motherwell	1-2	Aluko
Thu 22 May	RANGERS	2-0	Miller, Mackie

ABERDEEN FOOTBALL CLUB
MILESTONES

8TH OCTOBER 1881 The original Aberdeen formed after a public meeting held in the Albert Hall in Correction Wynd. Three teachers from Woodside School initiated the meeting and the secretary was instructed to purchase a ball, an inflator and eleven maroon jerseys.

2ND SEPTEMBER 1899 Aberdeen make their debut at Pittodrie—Dumbarton visited and are sent packing, 7-1. Alex Shiach became the first player to score at Pittodrie and he went on to net a hat-trick in this game.

14TH APRIL 1903 The current Aberdeen Football Club is formed by merging the three teams in the city, Aberdeen, Victoria United and Orion.

20TH AUGUST 1904 Aberdeen make their debut in League football with a 2-1 defeat at home to Falkirk. They wore a Black & Gold strip and were soon nicknamed the 'Wasps'.

MAY 1905 First Division football finally arrives at Pittodrie as the top division is expanded from 14 to 16.

APRIL 1930 Benny Yorston scores 38 goals from 38 league matches—a club record that still stands to this day. Yorston also scored six in the Scottish Cup that season.

NOVEMBER 1931 The 'Great Mystery' rocks Aberdeen - five players suddenly dropped after an alleged betting scandal was discovered. Hugh McLaren, Benny Yorston and Frank Hill would never play for the club again.

24TH APRIL 1937 A British record attendance of 146,433 fills Hampden for the Cup Final between Aberdeen and Celtic. The Black & Golds go down 2-1.

11TH MAY 1946 Aberdeen win the Southern League Cup after a remarkable 3-2 win over Rangers at Hampden. 135,000 see George Taylor score the winner in the last minute.

19TH APRIL 1947 Aberdeen finally win the Scottish Cup. Stan Williams scores the winner in a 2-1 win over Hibernian. Thousands gather at Aberdeen Station for the players return.

9TH APRIL 1955 Archie Glen's penalty winner against Clyde at Shawfield hands Aberdeen their first ever Scottish League title. Aberdeen 'A' also get in on the act by winning the reserve title.

22ND OCTOBER 1955 Aberdeen win the League Cup after defeating St Mirren 2-1 in the Hampden Final. 15,000 welcome the team on their return to Aberdeen Joint Station.

6TH SEPTEMBER 1967 Aberdeen play their first tie in European competition and register their club record 10-0 win over KR Reykjavik at Pittodrie in the ECWC.

11TH APRIL 1970 Aberdeen win the Scottish Cup for only the second time when they defeat Celtic 3-1. Derek McKay came from the reserves to play a starring role scoring the winner in both the quarter and semi finals and a brace in the Final. Martin Buchan becomes the youngest captain to lift the trophy.

30TH SEPTEMBER 1970 The Dons become the first team to go out of Europe on penalties, losing to Honved.

6TH NOVEMBER 1976 The Dons win the League Cup for the first time in 21 years – a first trophy for captain Willie Miller.

3RD MAY 1980 At Easter Road the Dons' clinch their first league title since 1955 by beating Hibernian 5-0.

22ND MAY 1982 The Dons crush Rangers 4-1 in the Scottish Cup Final, the highlight being a spectacular equaliser from Alex McLeish. The Dons also finished just behind Celtic in the league race, which went down to the final day of the season.

11TH MAY 1983 Gothenburg welcomes Aberdeen and Real Madrid for the ECWC Final. The Dons reach their pinnacle in a 2-1 win. John Hewitt added to Eric Black's early goal to spark wild scenes of jubilation all over Scotland. More than 16,000 of the Red Army at the Ullevi Stadium sing and dance in the rain.

21ST MAY 1983 Aberdeen do the double with another Scottish Cup win over Rangers. This time only an Eric Black header in extra time separates the sides.

DECEMBER 1983 Aberdeen beat European Cup holders Hamburg in the Super Cup

- more than 80 countries worldwide take in the game. Aberdeen named as European Team of the Year.

2ND MAY 1984 The Dons win the Premier title after a 1-0 win at Tynecastle. The Dons also retain the Scottish Cup after beating Celtic 2-1 in the Final.

27TH OCTOBER 1985 The last trophy to have eluded Alex Ferguson is won after the Dons beat Hibernian 3-0 in the League Cup Final at Hampden.

10TH MAY 1986 Aberdeen win their fourth Scottish Cup in five seasons beating Hearts 3-0.

22ND OCTOBER 1989 The Dons win the League Cup after two Paul Mason goals defeat Rangers – the last trophy win for captain Willie Miller.

12TH MAY 1990 The first ever Scottish Cup Final to be decided on penalties goes the way of Aberdeen - Theo Snelders and Brian Irvine are the Dons heroes in the shoot out.

26TH NOVEMBER 1995 The Dons win the League Cup after defeating Dundee 2-0 in the Final.

19TH MARCH 2000 Aberdeen lose out 2-0 to a superior Celtic in the CIS Cup Final. Thomas Solberg is sent off.

26TH MAY 2000 Jim Leighton is injured in the first minute of the Cup Final and with it goes any hope of Aberdeen winning the Scottish Cup. Aberdeen finish bottom of the SPL with a record 83 goals conceded. Dons saved due to SPL ground criteria.

SEPTEMBER 2007 Aberdeen return to European action after an absence of five years and qualify for the group stages of the UEFA Cup for the first time.

CROSSWORD

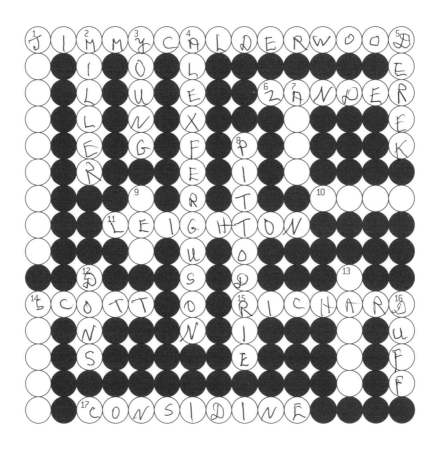

ACROSS

1   Meet the manager!
6   ___ Diamond
10 Central defender Lee ___
11 Aberdeen's greatest goalkeeper
14 ___ Severin
15 ___ Foster
17 Defender Andrew

DOWN

1   The great goalscorer of the 1970s
2   Top goalscorer last season
3 & 5 Midfielder who returned to the club last season
4   Our most successful manager ever
7 & 9 Our supporters
8   Where do we play
12 Our nickname
13 Ex-midfielder ___ Touzani
14 Jamie ___
16 Stuart who came from Dundee United

ANSWERS ON P61

WINNERS!

ABERDEEN HAVE WON PLENTY OF TROPHIES OVER OUR HISTORY – HERE'S OUR ROLL OF HONOUR!

HONOURS

European Cup Winners' Cup (1): 1982-83

European Super Cup (1): 1983-84

Scottish League Champions (4): 1954-55; 1979-80; 1983-84; 1984-85

Scottish Cup Winners (7): 1946-47; 1969-70; 1981-82; 1982-83; 1983-84; 1985-86; 1989-90

Scottish League Cup Winners (5): 1955-56; 1976-77; 1985-86; 1989-90; 1995-96

Southern League Cup Winners (1): 1946

Drybrough Cup Winners (2): 1971-72; 1980-81

CLUB RECORDS

First match: Aberdeen 1 - 1 Stenhousemuir (Pittodrie; August 15, 1903)

Largest win: Aberdeen 13 - 0 Peterhead (Pittodrie, Scottish Cup 3rd Round; February 10, 1923)

Largest defeat: Celtic 8 - 0 Aberdeen (Celtic Park, Scottish First Division; January 30, 1965)

Highest home attendance: 45,061 vs Hearts, Scottish Cup Quarter-final, 13 March 1954

Highest average home attendance: 24,200, 1948-49 (15 games)

Most capped player: Jim Leighton, 91 Scotland

Most League appearances: Willie Miller, 556, 1973-1990

Most goals scored: Joe Harper, 205

Most goals in a season: Benny Yorston, 38, 1934-35

Highest Transfer fee received: £1,750,000 Eoin Jess, Coventry City February 1996

Highest Transfer fee paid: £1,000,000 Paul Bernard, Oldham Athletic September 1995

HOME SWEET HOME

PITTODRIE HAS BEEN OUR HOME SINCE EVEN BEFORE THE CURRENT ABERDEEN FC WAS FORMED, SO IT'S REALLY AN HISTORIC MONUMENT!

It was opened on 2nd September 1899 when Alex Shiach scored the first goal, going on to hit a hat-trick in a 7-1 win over Dumbarton. Aberdeen FC as we know it today was founded in 1903 and continued to play at Pittodrie Park.

In 1908, Pittodrie staged its first Scottish Cup semi-final as Aberdeen battled their way through to meet Celtic. With no neutral venues in those days, Aberdeen were happy to take on Celtic at home. A record 20,000 crowd filled every vantage point but they were angry at the Celtic approach; robust and rough at best, downright brutal at their very worst. Celtic squeezed through 1-0 but that only upset the home support who barracked the Celtic players at every turn.

By 1920, capacity at Pittodrie was increased to 28,000 with work on the Main Stand beginning

to take shape and the embankment increased on the south side of the ground. A new record attendance was set in November 1919 when 25,000 turned out for the visit of Celtic. In September 1929, the days when Benny Yorston was scoring goals for fun, Aberdeen attracted 32,000 to Pittodrie for the visit of Rangers, the legendary Alex Cheyne scoring for the Dons in a 1-1 draw.

After World War II ended, it was common to see Pittodrie filled to capacity and the club record was again broken on 13th March 1954 when an incredible 45,061 attended the quarter final Scottish Cup replay against Hearts. The Dons responded in style in a slick 3-0 win.

Misfortune was to strike Pittodrie on the 6th February 1971. A fire destroyed part of the Main Stand, and gutted the dressing rooms and club

offices. The Scottish Cup – held by Aberdeen at the time – had to be rescued by firemen. Much of the club's history was lost that night and many people also feel the League title was lost that season as Celtic just pipped Aberdeen, the Dons' home form suffering after the fire.

The stadium had recovered though by November when it hosted two classic matches that drew attendances of over 30,000 in a week. The Dons took on Italian giants Juventus in the UEFA Cup while Scotland played their first international away from Hampden for 35 years when they took on Belgium at Pittodrie.

The last crowd in excess of 30,000 at Pittodrie was for the Scottish Cup tie against Rangers in 1975. That day it took a marvellous volley from a young Willie Miller to earn a deserved 1-1 draw before Aberdeen won the replay in Glasgow.

With stadium and safety requirements being paramount in the modern era, there is no chance of such crowds being brought back to the ground. Pittodrie has gradually been redeveloped and the capacity has been cut drastically to allow for all seating. On the 1st July 1979 Pittodrie became the first planned all-seated stadium in Great Britain after the south terracing, known locally as 'the ground', was fitted with bench style seats.

The most recent development of the stadium came in 1993 when the Beach End stand on the east side of the ground was demolished with the new Richard Donald Stand constructed in its place.

Pittodrie has 109 years of history in the bank already – and there are more memorable moments to come!

IMPROVE YOUR SKILLS WITH JAMIE SMITH!

1v1 FACING AN OPPONENT SIDESTEP

THE MOVE:
The player fakes to pass the ball with the outside of the foot but instead steps behind the ball and takes it in the opposite direction with the outside of the other foot.

COACHING POINTS:

- Use eyes and communication to disguise the pass

- Exaggerate upper body movement to deceive and unbalance the opponent

- Short step behind the ball is all that is required

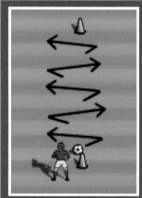

SKILL PRACTICE 1

- Players work moving forward in between the 2 cones practicing the side step move.
- Step right – go left
- Step left – go right
- See how many moves you can perform and try to beat your record.

SKILL PRACTICE 2

- Dribble forward to cones and perform the left go right side step then drive forward to opposite cone.
- Repeat exercise this time performing the right go left move.
- Progression – try double side step
- Step right – left – right
- Step left – right – left

PLAYERS MUST BE AWARE OF THE VARIOUS SITUATIONS ON THE PARK

WHERE & WHEN THE MOVE CAN BE BEST EXECUTED:

- STRIKER – When in or around the box and confronted with a defender face to face, using a quick side step move will allow you to create space to finish on goal.

- MIDFIELDER – When attacking at an angle from a wide midfield position and being faced with an opponent, a quick side step move will allow you to create space for a penetrating pass, a cross or shot at goal.

- DEFENDER – When being faced by an opponent in a defending area performing a quick side step move will allow you space to set up a forward pass into midfielder/striker or winger enabling you to set up an attack from a defensive situation.

CHRIS MAGUIRE
THE YOUTH OF TODAY!

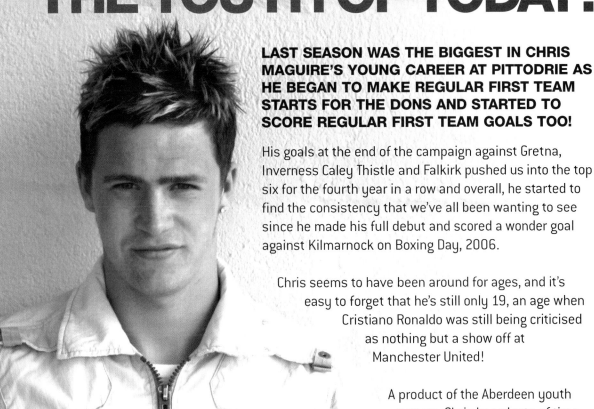

LAST SEASON WAS THE BIGGEST IN CHRIS MAGUIRE'S YOUNG CAREER AT PITTODRIE AS HE BEGAN TO MAKE REGULAR FIRST TEAM STARTS FOR THE DONS AND STARTED TO SCORE REGULAR FIRST TEAM GOALS TOO!

His goals at the end of the campaign against Gretna, Inverness Caley Thistle and Falkirk pushed us into the top six for the fourth year in a row and overall, he started to find the consistency that we've all been wanting to see since he made his full debut and scored a wonder goal against Kilmarnock on Boxing Day, 2006.

Chris seems to have been around for ages, and it's easy to forget that he's still only 19, an age when Cristiano Ronaldo was still being criticised as nothing but a show off at Manchester United!

A product of the Aberdeen youth system, Chris has plenty of time on his side and shows all the signs that he can go on and become a legend for the Dons over the next few years.

WHICH WAY?

GARY MCDONALD HASN'T BEEN WITH THE DONS FOR LONG, AND HE STILL CAN'T WORK OUT HOW TO GET FROM THE TRAINING GROUND TO THE DRESSING ROOM AT PITTODRIE.

CAN YOU HELP HIM FIND THE WAY?

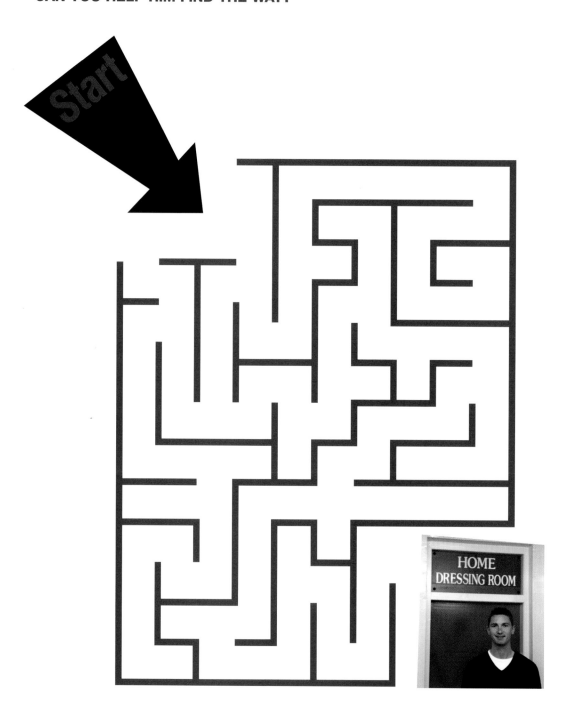

ANSWER p61

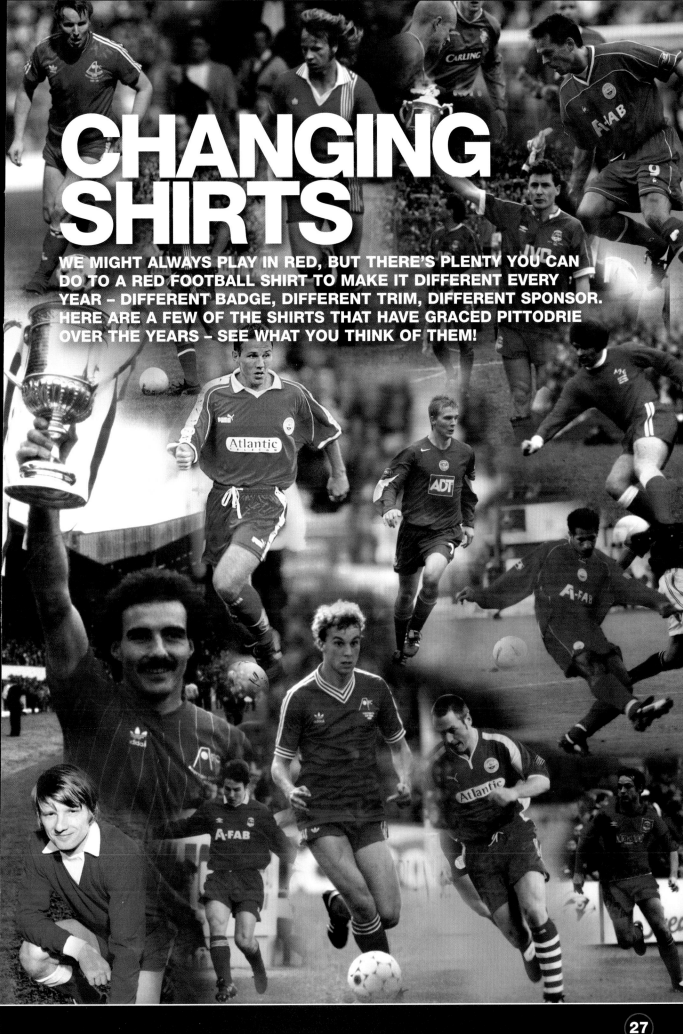

CHANGING SHIRTS

WE MIGHT ALWAYS PLAY IN RED, BUT THERE'S PLENTY YOU CAN DO TO A RED FOOTBALL SHIRT TO MAKE IT DIFFERENT EVERY YEAR – DIFFERENT BADGE, DIFFERENT TRIM, DIFFERENT SPONSOR. HERE ARE A FEW OF THE SHIRTS THAT HAVE GRACED PITTODRIE OVER THE YEARS – SEE WHAT YOU THINK OF THEM!

Q&A ZANDER DIAMOND

What is your favourite ice-cream?
LEMON MERINGUE

What was your best and worst subject at school?
BEST – CRAFT & DESIGN. WORST – ENGLISH

Who did you have a schoolboy crush on?
PAMELA ANDERSON

If you could buy a ticket for any event in the world, what would it be?
WORLD CUP FINAL

What would your superpower be?
TO BE INVISIBLE

What is your most treasured possession?
PLAYSTATION 3

What is your favourite TV programme?
RIVER CITY

What is the best film ever made?
DUMB & DUMBER

Who is your favourite cartoon character?
HOMER SIMPSON

What is your favourite computer game?
FOOTBALL MANAGER

What was the last song/album you downloaded to your iPod?
REAL McCOY – ANOTHER NIGHT

Who would play you in the film of your life?
JIM CAREY

What keeps you awake at night?
THINKING ABOUT THE FUTURE

What is your favourite item of clothing?
PROBABLY TRAINERS, GOT OVER 30 PAIRS

What type/make of football boots do you wear?
PUMA KONSTRUKT II

What is your greatest achievement in football?
PROBABLY REACHING LAST 32 IN THE UEFA CUP v BAYERN MUNICH

What is your favourite goal you have scored?
LOKOMOTIV MOSCOW IN THE UEFA CUP

Have you any pre-match rituals?
ALWAYS EAT TOAST & HONEY

When was the last time you used public transport?
CAN'T REMEMBER, IT'S BEEN THAT LONG....

Who is your best friend in the dressing room?
IT WAS DEREK SOUTER

IMPROVE YOUR SKILLS
WITH JEFFREY DE VISSCHER

1v1
DIAGONAL ATTACK
DRAG BACK FLICK

THE MOVE:
When the attacking player is challenged diagonally from the side the player drags the ball back past the heel of the standing leg and then taps the ball behind the leg with the inside of the drag back foot.

COACHING POINTS:
• Fake to strike the ball before dragging it back.
• Position your body between the challenging player and the ball. This shields and protects the ball.
• The drag back foot is always furthest from the opponent.
• After tapping the ball behind the standing leg accelerate out of the move.

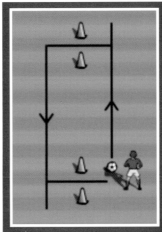

SKILL PRACTICE 1
• Dribble forward and perform the right foot de Visscher move in between the two cones.
• After the move dribble back and perform the same move in between the next two cones.
• Stop the ball initially when practicing then practice the move without stopping the ball.
• Progression: Repeat practice in opposite direction using the left foot.

SKILL PRACTICE 2
FAST FEET SKILL PRACTICE
• Set out 5 markers at an overall distance of 4 meters.
• Work up the circuit using right foot (RF) and left foot (LF) de Visscher moves.
• After a few practices start timing how long it takes. Try and beat your record each time.

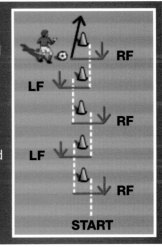

PLAYERS MUST BE AWARE OF THE VARIOUS SITUATIONS ON THE PARK

WHERE & WHEN THE MOVE CAN BE BEST EXECUTED:

• STRIKER – When being pressurised by a defender from the side in a good attacking position in or around the 18 yard box, performing the de Visscher move will allow you to create space for a strike at goal.

• MIDFIELDER – When driving forward from midfield and confronted by defenders the de Visscher move can be used to tap the ball into the path of any oncoming team mate, who can either shoot for goal or make a pass into the strikers.

• DEFENDER – When being closed down from the side and facing your own goal in a wide defensive position, producing the de Visscher drag back will create space to set up a new attacking situation.

ANGUS' MOUTHWATERING ROCK 'N' ROLL CAKE RECIPE

INGREDIENTS TO MAKE ABOUT 24 OF ANGUS' SPECIAL ROCK'N'ROLL CAKES:

300G PLAIN FLOUR
100G BUTTER
100G SUGAR

1/2 CUP RAISINS
1 EGG
RED FOOD COLOURING (OPTIONAL)

METHOD:

Ask a grown up to turn the oven on to 200 C / 400 F / gas mark 6 and make sure you've got a lightly greased baking tray ready. You can grease the tray if it's ok!

Tip the flour into a large mixing bowl and then add the butter. This is where it gets messy - hurrah! Using your fingers, crumble the butter into the flour. This may take a few minutes and the mixture will then start to turn into fine crumbs.

When you are happy with your mixture, add the sugar and then the raisins - you can eat one raisin now if you're really, really hungry! Mix all the ingredients together.

Add a beaten egg to the mixture, then add a few drops of red food colouring (let the grown up supervise this and only add it if you want the cakes to be red – it won't change the flavour if you leave it out).

Mix it all together with your hands and form the dough into small round balls. Place them carefully on to the baking tray and ask the grown up to put them in the oven for 15 minutes.

When time is up, get the grown up to take them out of the oven, but make sure you leave them to cool before you touch them because they're hot! As soon as they've cooled a little, get stuck in! Leave a few for Angus though!

IMPROVE YOUR SKILLS WITH RICHARD FOSTER

1v1 SIDE BY SIDE (STOP TURN)

THE MOVE:

The Player dribbles forward jumps over the ball and stops ball with sole of the foot. After landing beyond the ball turn quickly and take the ball away in the opposite direction.

Practice this move at least 10 times each day for a minimum of 5 days a week.

COACHING POINTS:

• Do not hesitate when jumping over the ball.

• Use light touch with the sole of the foot when stopping the ball.

• After changing direction accelerate out of the move.

SKILL PRACTICE

• In this practice the 2 cones in the middle ACT AS THE OPPOSING PLAYERS.

• To start, dribble with the ball to the 3rd cone where the player is on your right hand side.

• Perform the left foot turn to change direction.

• Then dribble back to the 2nd cone and change direction again this time using the right foot turn.

• Once you have performed the turn dribble forward to the 4th cone and repeat practice.

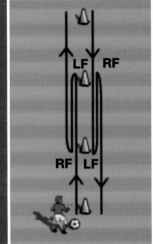

TO USE THIS MOVE EFFECTIVELY IT HAS TO BE PRACTICED REGULARLY WITH BOTH FEET.

WHERE & WHEN THE MOVE CAN BE BEST EXECUTED:

• STRIKER - driving across edge of the box with opponent side by side performs the turn to create space for shot at goal.

• MIDFIELDER - driving across midfield can change direction quickly to switch play or pass to striker to create opening.

• DEFENDER - running back towards own goal under pressure from opposition can change direction quickly to create space and start attacking.

ALL HAIL THE GOTHENBURG GREATS!

Only one Scottish team has won two European trophies — us! So when the 25th anniversary of our European Cup Winners' Cup win in Gothenburg in 1983 rolled around, it was only right that we marked the occasion with a special testimonial match so we could all show our appreciation for the guys who carried away the silverware all those years ago.

The Gothenburg Greats even got out on the pitch to remind us of those twinkling feet — even if the passing years have been kinder to some of them than others!

To mark the day, the main event was the return of the manager from 1983, Sir Alex Ferguson, who brought a full strength Manchester United team to Pittodrie to show his respect for his players who achieved so much back then and put Aberdeen on the football map forever.

In front of a packed Pittodrie, United and the Dons played out a closely fought game, United just finding enough to win thanks to a Michael Carrick penalty and a header from Wayne Rooney.

But the day was all about the Gothenburg Greats. As Sir Alex said afterwards, "Never forget what they achieved!"

BETWEEN THE POSTS

The Dons have had plenty of great goalkeepers since the club came into being in 1903. The first really big name in goal was Fred Martin who started his career as a striker before being converted to goalkeeper! Fred was in goal when Aberdeen won the league title for the first time in 1954/55 and in the victorious League Cup Final a year later, as well as ending up on the losing side three times in the Scottish Cup Final. He also won six caps for Scotland during his Aberdeen career.

Bobby Clark is another all time Aberdeen great after a 17 year stay at Pittodrie where he amassed 17 Scotland caps too and went to the 1978 World Cup in Argentina. Bobby completed the clean sweep of titles in Scotland, winning the Scottish Cup in 1970, the League Cup in 1976 and, finally, the Premier Division title in 1980 before he was replaced by the man who is unquestionably Aberdeen's greatest goalkeeper, Jim Leighton.

Jim was part of the legendary "Gothenburg Greats" side that won the European Cup Winners' Cup in 1983 and then the UEFA Super Cup as well. Add to that four Scottish Cups, three Premier League titles and two League Cups and it's obvious how important Jim was at Pittodrie. And he still is, taking charge of his successors as the club's goalkeeping coach. Leighton also won 91 caps for Scotland, a record that is second only to Kenny Dalglish.

Following Jim was no easy task, but when Leighton left for Manchester United – he came back home later in his career – Dutchman Theo Snelders stepped into the breach and did a pretty decent job! He was voted PFA Player of the Year in 1989 and then in 1990 he became a legend at Pittodrie by saving a penalty in the Scottish Cup Final shootout with Celtic, helping the Dons lift the cup.

Jamie Langfield is the man in possession of the number one shirt at the moment, having seen off plenty of competition during his four years here at Pittodrie. Jamie has played more than 100 games for the club and, at only 28, will have his best years ahead of him, goalkeepers tending to get better with age. He'll still have to go some to catch up with Bobby Clark or Jim Leighton's appearance records though!

WEARING THE COLOURS

STUART DUFF AND LEE MAIR ARE LOOKING A BIT UNDERDRESSED –
SO LET YOUR IMAGINATION GO WILD AND COME UP WITH A COUPLE
OF NEW KITS FOR THE DONS.

HOME, AWAY, IT DOESN'T MATTER, JUST MAKE THEM THE BEST
DRESSED PLAYERS IN THE SPL!

IMPROVE YOUR SKILLS WITH LEE MILLER

1v1 DIAGONAL ATTACK DRAG BACK

THE MOVE:
When being challenged from the side fake to strike the ball but instead drag the ball back with the sole of the same foot and push off in the opposite direction using the inside or outside of the drag back foot.

Coaching Points:
• Exaggerate the fake strike of the ball
• Drag back must be executed quickly
• Get ball out of feet to clear the incoming opponent
• To be successful the timing of the move is crucial

SKILL PRACTICE 1

• Dribble the ball slightly past the left hand cone and perform the right foot (RF) drag back move.
• Then dribble across to the other cone and perform the left foot (LF) drag back. Dribble through the middle of the two cones.
• Stop the ball and repeat the practice.

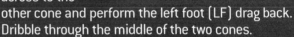

SKILL PRACTICE 2

• Start at the first cone by performing the right foot (RF) drag back.
• Proceed to the second cone and perform the left foot (LF) drag back.
• Continue up the circuit using the right foot and left foot drag back move.

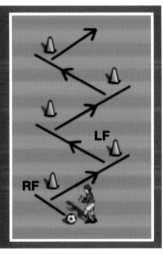

PLAYERS MUST BE AWARE OF THE VARIOUS SITUATIONS ON THE PARK

WHERE & WHEN THE MOVE CAN BE BEST EXECUTED:

• STRIKER – When driving forward into the box and being challenged diagonally from the side using the drag back move will allow the player to create space to beat the defender, creating an opportunity to finish on goal.

• MIDFIELDER – When dribbling forward in a midfield position and being challenged diagonally from the side, quickly performing the drag back move will allow the player to create space for a pass into the striker or wide player.

• DEFENDER – When in possession of the ball outside the penalty box and facing your own goal the drag back move would be a good option when being challenged from the side. The move would allow the player to create space and take the ball clear of the danger zone.

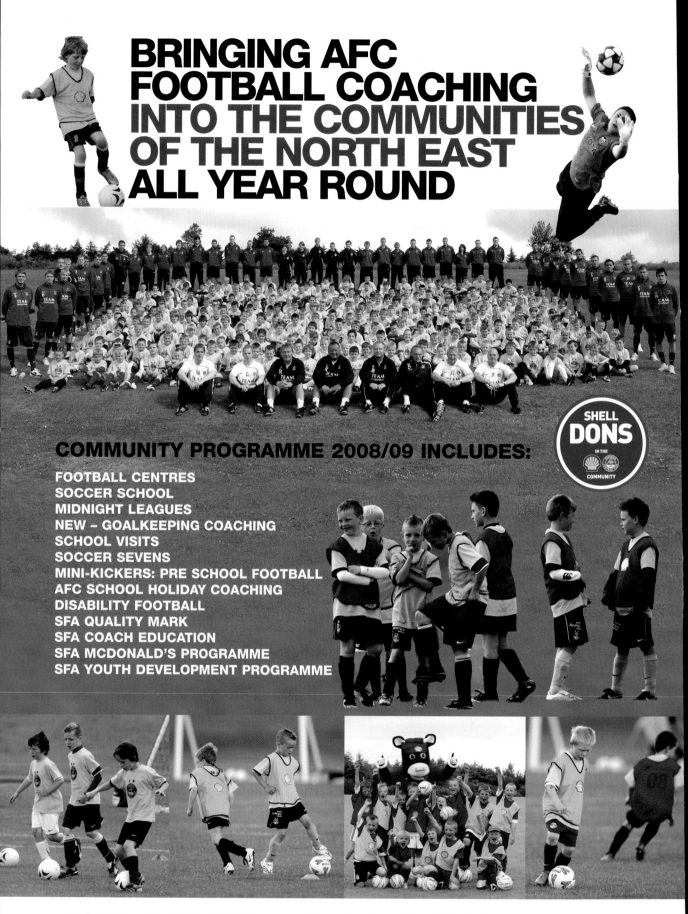

BRINGING AFC FOOTBALL COACHING INTO THE COMMUNITIES OF THE NORTH EAST ALL YEAR ROUND

COMMUNITY PROGRAMME 2008/09 INCLUDES:

FOOTBALL CENTRES
SOCCER SCHOOL
MIDNIGHT LEAGUES
NEW – GOALKEEPING COACHING
SCHOOL VISITS
SOCCER SEVENS
MINI-KICKERS: PRE SCHOOL FOOTBALL
AFC SCHOOL HOLIDAY COACHING
DISABILITY FOOTBALL
SFA QUALITY MARK
SFA COACH EDUCATION
SFA MCDONALD'S PROGRAMME
SFA YOUTH DEVELOPMENT PROGRAMME

SHELL DONS IN THE COMMUNITY

FOR MORE INFORMATION CALL 01224 650472/650432
OR VISIT WWW.AFC.CO.UK/COMMUNITY

Join the

ANGUS THE BULL CLUB!

sponsored by
BIBBY
OFFSHORE LIMITED

ISS

Membership is free and open to any young AFC fan aged 12 or under. Benefits include:

+ *Exclusive ATBC membership gift*
+ *VIP Invitation to an ATBC party*
+ *Dedicated ATBC members section of RedWeb with loads of great offers, downloads and games*
+ *Great competitions, including the chance to become "Little Gus"!*

To join visit www.afc.co.uk

Y★★URCITY
YOURTEAM

Q&A MICHAEL PATON

What is your favourite ice-cream?
MINT CHOC-CHIP

What was your best and worst subject at school?
BEST – PE. WORST – GRAPHIC COMMUNICATION

Who did you have a schoolboy crush on?
BABY SPICE

If you could buy a ticket for any event in the world,
what would it be?
CHAMPIONS LEAGUE FINAL

What would your superpower be?
TO BE INVISIBLE

What is your most treasured possession?
PHONE

What is your favourite TV programme?
SUNDAY NIGHT PROJECT

What is the best film ever made?
SHAWSHANK REDEMPTION

Who is your favourite cartoon character?
PETER GRIFFIN (FAMILY GUY)

What is your favourite computer game?
PRO EVOLUTION – FOOTBALL MANAGER

What was the last song/album you downloaded to your iPod?
BASEHUNTER – ALL I EVER WANTED

Who would play you in the film of your life?
PETER GRIFFIN

What keeps you awake at night?
THE LIGHT ON

What is your favourite item of clothing?
MY JEANS

What type/make of football boots do you wear?
ADIDAS WHITE PREDATORS

What is your greatest achievement in football?
**PLAYING AGAINST
MANCHESTER UNITED**

What is your favourite goal you have scored?
**1ST GOAL FOR BRECHIN LAST
SEASON WHEN I WAS ON LOAN**

Have you any pre-match rituals?
LISTEN TO MUSIC

When was the last time you used public transport?
CAN'T REMEMBER

Who is your best friend in the dressing room?
**GET ON WELL WITH EVERYONE, BUT I AM ALWAYS
HANGING ABOUT WITH STU SMITH AND SAMMY STEWART**

CAPTAINS SCARLET!

Aberdeen have had plenty of great leaders over the years, but a few really stand out from the crowd, **FRANK DUNLOP** the first, leading the Dons to their first successes on the national stage, captaining the side that beat Rangers 3-2 in the Southern League Cup Final before a 153,000 Hampden crowd. A year later, the Scottish Cup followed after a win over Hibernian.

JIMMY MITCHELL was a record club buy from Morton in 1952 who went on to lead Aberdeen through a successful period and was captain for Scottish Cup finals of 1953 and 1954 and was skipper as Aberdeen won a first League Championship in 1955 and then the League Cup later that year. Mitchell was famed for his television interview after the final when he invited all Aberdonians to a party in Aberdeen. More than 15,000 took him up on his offer as the Aberdeen Joint Station was swamped late into the night as the victorious Aberdeen side returned with the cup!

MARTIN BUCHAN was a surprise choice of captain in 1970. His first game as captain was certainly an eventful one as the Dons were jeered from the Pittodrie pitch after scraping past Clydebank in a Scottish Cup tie. Two months later Buchan became the youngest player to captain a cup winning side when Aberdeen defeated Celtic 3-1 at Hampden to lift the Scottish Cup. Buchan remains the youngest winning captain to this day.

WILLIE MILLER became the youngest ever Aberdeen captain and his period in command was the most successful in the Dons' history. Miller served under Ally MacLeod, Billy McNeill, Alex Ferguson, Ian Porterfield and Alex Smith in a career that brought unprecedented success to the club. His first win was the League Cup in 1976 and there followed three Premier League titles, four Scottish Cups, two more League Cups and the European Cup Winners' Cup in 1983. Miller rounded off a glorious spell as captain in 1989 when Aberdeen defeated Rangers 2-1 at Hampden to lift the League Cup. Later that season after Willie had sustained an injury that effectively ended his playing career, **ALEX MCLEISH** took over as captain and led Aberdeen to a Scottish Cup win in 1990 over Celtic.

RUSSELL ANDERSON took over the job in 2003 and was outstanding in the role before his move to Sunderland which left the way for **SCOTT SEVERIN** to start doing the job. He's in his second season now, so get behind Seve and the boys!

THE BIG QUIZ

1 With which club did Lee Miller begin his career?

2 Who was last season's top goalscorer?

3 And how many goals did he score?

4 Which Aberdeen goalkeeper used to play for West Bromwich Albion?

5 Who is Derek Young's footballing brother?

6 Which company sponsors the Dons?

7 What nationality is Jeffrey de Visscher?

8 Which other Scottish team has Jamie Smith played for?

9 What is special about squad number 12?

10 How many times did Jim Leighton play for Scotland?

11 In what year did Aberdeen win their first League Championship?

12 Last season Aberdeen celebrated the 25th Anniversary of which event?

13 Aberdeen are the only Scottish club to have won two European trophies. Name them?

14 Who did Aberdeen defeat in 1983 to win the European Super Cup?

15 Which German side knocked Aberdeen out of last season's UEFA Cup?

16 Name the ex-Aberdeen player who played in last season's FA Cup Final?

17 How many times have Aberdeen won the Scottish Cup?

18 What was the last trophy Aberdeen won and in what year?

19 How many games did Aberdeen play in total last season?

20 Name the ex-Aberdeen player who scored the winning goal in last season's English Championship Play off game at Wembley?

21 How many years in a row has Aberdeen's official matchday programme been named the best in the SPL?

22 Gary McDonald scored the winning goal for Oldham against which Premiership side in the FA Cup last season?

23 Jimmy Nicholl was manager of which club when they won the League Cup against Celtic?

24 Which club did Aberdeen born players Lee Mair and Stuart Duff play for?

25 Name the three players in picture A.

A

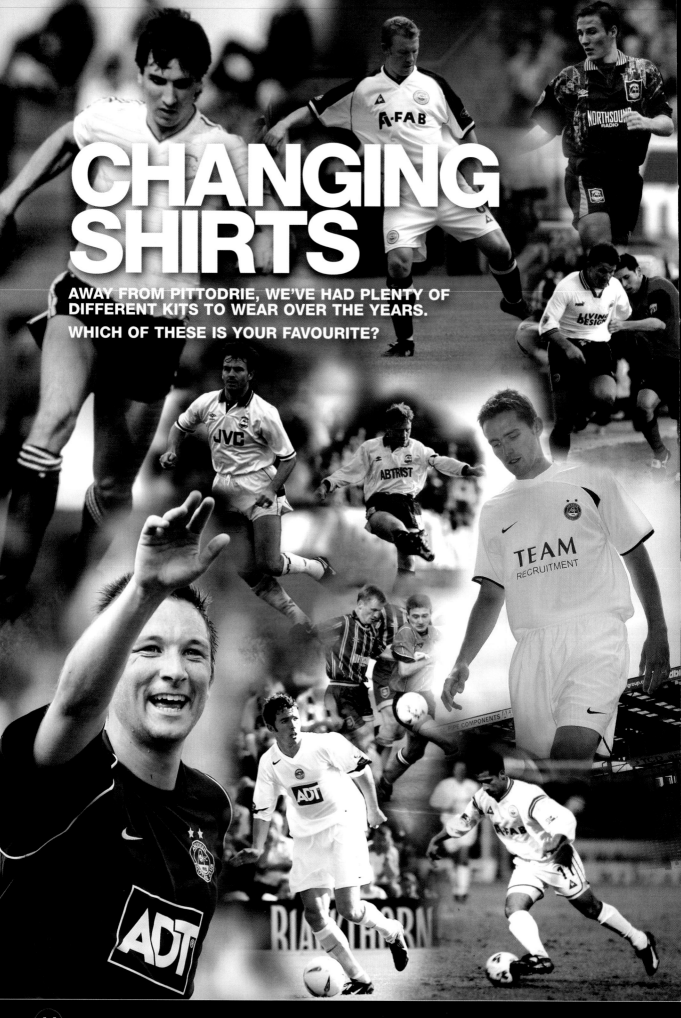

CHANGING SHIRTS

AWAY FROM PITTODRIE, WE'VE HAD PLENTY OF DIFFERENT KITS TO WEAR OVER THE YEARS.

WHICH OF THESE IS YOUR FAVOURITE?

IMPROVE YOUR SKILLS WITH DEREK YOUNG!

SKILL PRACTICE 1

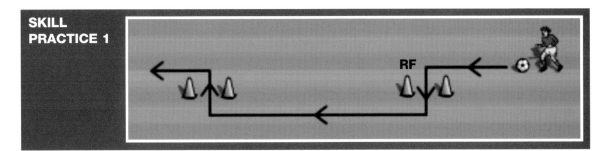

FLICK BEHIND STANDING LEG

THE MOVE:
Whilst dribbling at pace with opponent alongside flick the ball behind the standing leg using the front part of the sole or the inside of the foot to create space and time.

COACHING POINTS:
- Shield the ball on opposite side of opponent.
- Flick or roll the ball behind the standing leg at a slight angle to create more space.
- Change direction quickly.

SKILL PRACTICE 2

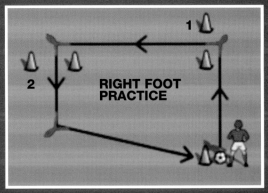

- In skill practice 2 the player dribbles to first set of cones 1 and performs the right foot move.
- The player continues on and repeats the move at second set of cones 2.
- The player then quickly performs another right foot move before returning to the starting point.

SKILL PRACTICE 3

- For skill practice 3 follow the above instructions but this time using the left foot move.

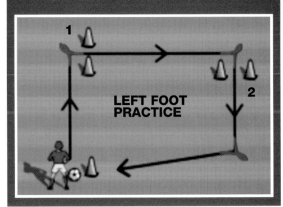

HE'S THE GREATEST!

THERE AREN'T MANY FOOTBALL MANAGERS WHO HAVE A SUCCESS STORY TO TELL LIKE SIR ALEX FERGUSON – AND IT ALL STARTED HERE AT PITTODRIE!

Under Fergie, the Dons won trophy after trophy, most notably two European competitions, the Cup Winners' Cup and the Super Cup, making Aberdeen the most successful club from Scotland in European competition.

After he left Aberdeen, he went on to even greater achievements with Manchester United, but he has always had a soft spot for his old club, hence his return here in July, bringing his full team to pay tribute to the side of 1983 and to entertain the Aberdeen fans one more time.

All hail Sir Alex – he's the greatest!

Q&A SAMMY STEWART

What is your favourite ice-cream?
BELGIAN CHOCOLATE

What was your best and worst subject at school?
BEST – P.E. WORST – HISTORY

Who did you have a schoolboy crush on?
CHRISTINA AGUILERA

If you could buy a ticket for any event in the world, what would it be?
EITHER THE CHAMPIONS LEAGUE FINAL OR THE WORLD CUP FINAL

What would your superpower be?
PROBABLY THE ABILITY TO FLY

What is your most treasured possession?
PHONE & FOOTBALL BOOTS

What is your favourite TV programme?
SOUTH PARK / PRISON BREAK / FRIENDS

What is the best film ever made?
TROY OR THE MATRIX OR A COMEDY SUCH AS TEAM AMERICA

Who is your favourite cartoon character?
SIMBA FROM THE LION KING OR CARTMAN FROM SOUTH PARK

What is your favourite computer game?
PRO EVOLUTION – FOOTBALL MANAGER

What was the last song/album you downloaded to your iPod?
NOT SURE PROBABLY NE-YO – CLOSER

Who would play you in the film of your life?
BRAD PITT

What keeps you awake at night?
TRAFFIC NOISE

What is your favourite item of clothing?
JEANS OR SHOES

What type/make of football boots do you wear?
ADIDAS

What is your greatest achievement in football?
SIGNING PRO FOR ABERDEEN & PLAYING AGAINST MANCHESTER UNITED

What is your favourite goal you have scored?
IT WOULD HAVE TO BE THE ONE AGAINST CLIFTONVILLE FOR MY OLD TEAM GLENAVON

Have you any pre-match rituals?
LISTENING TO MUSIC

When was the last time you used public transport?
A FEW DAYS AGO

Who is your best friend in the dressing room?
I GET ON WITH EVERYONE. MICK (MICHAEL PATON) & STUARTY (STUART SMITH) MAINLY BECAUSE THEY'RE AROUND MY AGE

PLAYER PROFILES

JAMIE LANGFIELD

BORN: 22 DECEMBER 1979
POSITION: GOALKEEPER
ABERDEEN APPEARANCES: 102

Jamie has been at Pittodrie since the summer of 2005 and has had to see off the challenge of a number of goalkeepers in his time here, including Derek Soutar over the last couple of years.

The former Dunfermline, Partick, Raith and Dundee stopper played a big part in the UEFA Cup campaign last season, and finished the campaign as the unquestioned number one, a position he will be looking to maintain this year.

ZANDER DIAMOND
BORN: 12 MARCH 1985
POSITION: CENTRE-HALF
ABERDEEN APPEARANCES: 144+13
ABERDEEN GOALS: 11

Still only 23, Zander has racked up well over 150 games for the Dons in his short career, having been hailed as the new Alex McLeish when he first came into the side, which is a big thing to burden any young player with!

Zander has had his ups and downs at Pittodrie in the last few years, but he was outstanding throughout last season and could well be a future captain of the club, as well as a possible international for Scotland.

BERTRAND BOSSU
BORN: 14 OCTOBER 1980
POSITION: GOALKEEPER
ABERDEEN APPEARANCES: 0

Bertrand joined the Dons last summer, the Frenchman coming to play in the SPL for the first time after having spent the last eight years playing south of the border for clubs such as Gillingham, Walsall, Darlington and Hayes, where he also turned up at the other end of the field to score a late goal in a game against St Albans City.

At 6 feet 7 inches tall, Bertrand should certainly be the boss of his penalty area!

RICHARD FOSTER
BORN: 31 JULY 1985
POSITION: FULL-BACK
ABERDEEN APPEARANCES: 112+55
ABERDEEN GOALS: 8

Proof that Aberdeen have a very young squad these days comes when you realise that Richard is one of the veterans here at Pittodrie – and he's only 23! He made his first appearances at the end of 2002/3 and has been in and around the first team ever since.

Versatile, Richard can play in midfield as well as the back and he likes to get forward too – he made the cross for Darren Mackie to head the winner in Dnipro and then got on the scoresheet himself in the 4-0 win over Copenhagen last season.

ANDREW CONSIDINE
BORN: 1 APRIL 1987
POSITION: CENTRE-HALF
ABERDEEN APPEARANCES: 72+17
ABERDEEN GOALS: 6

Andrew made his mark as a very promising young player once again last season, starting with Scotland's Under 20s at the World Cup in Canada and finishing as pretty much a regular in the first team under Jimmy Calderwood.

Still learning his trade at the back, he gets better with every game while he is also a very handy player to have at the opposite end of the field for set pieces as his goals in last season's cup ties proved.

CHARLIE MULGREW
BORN: 6 MARCH 1983
POSITION: FULL-BACK
ABERDEEN APPEARANCES: 0
ABERDEEN GOALS: 0

A Scotland Under-21 international in the past, Charlie is a product of the Celtic youth system who got his first taste of senior games during a loan spell at Dundee United. From there he joined Wolverhampton Wanderers, also having a loan spell at Southend United.

He signed for the Dons last summer and will now be looking to kick start his career by holding down a regular place in the side at left-back over the course of this season.

LEE MAIR
BORN: 9 DECEMBER 1980
POSITION: CENTRE-HALF
ABERDEEN APPEARANCES: 18+6
ABERDEEN GOALS: 1

Lee came back home when he signed for the Dons in the summer of 2007, returning to the town of his birth, though he had never played for Aberdeen before. He started his career at Dundee, playing for East Fife and Falkirk on loan before moving to Stockport County and then back to Dundee United.

A few minor injuries meant he had a difficult first year at Pittodrie but his ability and experience will be important qualities for the side this term.

GARY MCDONALD
BORN: 10 APRIL 1982
POSITION: MIDFIELD
ABERDEEN APPEARANCES: 0
ABERDEEN GOALS: 0

Gary was Jimmy Calderwood's first signing for this season, bringing him back to Scotland after the former Kilmarnock midfielder had enjoyed two seasons in England with Oldham Athletic.

The goalscoring midfielder made a national name for himself last season when he scored the goal that knocked Everton out of the FA Cup and now he hopes to enjoy similar cup fighting success with the Dons.

SCOTT SEVERIN
BORN: 15 FEBRUARY 1979
POSITION: MIDFIELD
ABERDEEN APPEARANCES: 149+3
ABERDEEN GOALS: 11

Seve had the unenviable job of replacing Russell Anderson as club captain last season but grew into the job as the campaign went on and led the side from the front all over the continent as we had our best European campaign in a generation.

Having twice missed out on a Hampden cup final, Seve will be looking to go one better this season and become the first skipper to lift a trophy for the Dons since 1996 when we won the League Cup.

DEREK YOUNG

BORN: 27 MAY 1980
POSITION: MIDFIELD
ABERDEEN APPEARANCES: 132+37
ABERDEEN GOALS: 17

Derek made a shock return to Pittodrie at the start of the 2007/8 season having left the club for Dunfermline, along with his brother Darren, back in 2003.

He won over any doubters by making a big contribution to the team, especially in the first half of the season before a number of injuries reduced his appearances in the last few months.

MARK KERR

BORN: 2 MARCH 1982
POSITION: MIDFIELD
ABERDEEN APPEARANCES: 0
ABERDEEN GOALS: 0

Like Gary McDonald and Bertrand Bossu, Mark was another summer signing to bolster the Aberdeen squad, joining the Dons after five years at Dundee United, following a similar period at Falkirk.

A solid presence in midfield usually playing just in front of the back four, Mark has played over 300 senior games at the age of 26, so his experience as he comes to the best years of his career should be invaluable for Jimmy Calderwood's team.

JEFFREY DE VISSCHER
BORN: 5 MAY 1981
POSITION: MIDFIELD
ABERDEEN APPEARANCES: 17+13
ABERDEEN GOALS: 3

Coming to play in the SPL was a little bit of a culture shock for Jeffrey at first, but the Dutchman quickly got used to the different challenge and pace of the game after joining from De Graafschap.

By the end of the season, he was producing his best form of the season, proving that by striking a crucial goal against Celtic in the Scottish Cup in front of a packed Pittodrie Stadium.

STUART DUFF
BORN: 23 JANUARY 1982
POSITION: MIDFIELD
ABERDEEN APPEARANCES: 7+4
ABERDEEN GOALS: 0

Another import from Tannadice, Stuart came to Pittodrie on a short term contract in January 2008 but did enough over the rest of the season to impress the management and earn himself a new contract with the club.

Adding to the competition for places in the midfield, Stuart took time to settle at Pittodrie but showed his best form in the closing weeks of the season, suggesting that there is plenty to come from him this term.

LEE MILLER
BORN: 18 MAY 1983
POSITION: STRIKER
ABERDEEN APPEARANCES: 74+11
ABERDEEN GOALS: 17

Lee has become a favourite over his two years at Pittodrie and he delighted the supporters by agreeing a new two year deal at the end of last season, a year where he finished as top scorer at the club with 13 goals.

Big and strong, Lee leads the line as well as anyone in the SPL and was a great capture when he joined from Dundee United for £225,000. An old fashioned centre-forward, Lee will be a very important player for the Dons as they look to get back into Europe this year.

DARREN MACKIE
BORN: 5 JANUARY 1982
POSITION: STRIKER
ABERDEEN APPEARANCES: 180+74
ABERDEEN GOALS: 53

Darren had a very difficult 2007/8 because of injury, missing a huge chunk of the season and only managed three goals as a result – but what important goals they were!

The first one, scored in the Ukraine, put the Dons into the group stage of the UEFA Cup for the first time ever, then his second, at Parkhead, saw Aberdeen through to the semi-final of the Scottish Cup. Finally, on the last day of the season, he netted against Rangers to ensure the season finished on a high with Aberdeen securing fourth place in the SPL.

JAMIE SMITH
BORN: 20 NOVEMBER 1980
POSITION: STRIKER
ABERDEEN APPEARANCES: 83+3
ABERDEEN GOALS: 18

There are few more influential players in the SPL than Jamie Smith and his injury problems last term certainly disrupted the team's results. At his best, Jamie is a real match winner for the Dons as he showed with a virtuoso performance against FC Copenhagen as Aberdeen made it through to the knock-out stages of the UEFA Cup.

A player for the big occasion, if Jamie can stay fit and play his part through the campaign, the Dons will be sure of having a great season.

CHRIS MAGUIRE:
BORN: 16 JANUARY 1989
POSITION: STRIKER
ABERDEEN APPEARANCES: 19+39
ABERDEEN GOALS: 5

A bit like Zander Diamond, Chris has been the victim of high expectations ever since he crashed in a goal on his full debut against Kilmarnock. Though he seems to have been around for ages, Chris is still only 19 and has barely begun his real football education at SPL level.

Making more and more starts as last season went on, there's evidence that Chris is maturing into a player who will make a huge contribution up front for the Dons in the years to come.

STUART SMITH:
BORN: 6 JULY 1989
POSITION: LEFT BACK
ABERDEEN APPEARANCES: 0

Stuart Smith joined the senior ranks this year after being promoted from the U19 side. The defender has always impressed here and did very well when he played for neighbours Peterhead on loan for the second half of last season.

The Fraserburgh born lad is one of the few players in the team who was born in the area. Although that puts a bit of extra pressure on Stuart it also means he has normally lots of friends and family in the crowd to give him support!

JOHN BATEMAN:
BORN: 3 JUNE 1989
POSITION: GOALKEEPER
ABERDEEN APPEARANCES: 0

John joined Aberdeen in the 2007/08 season after having come through the youth system at West Bromwich Albion. He was consistently impressive for the Under 19s last season and won deserved promotion to the first team squad for the 2008/9 campaign.

From a footballing family, John is related to Len Millard, West Brom's 1954 FA Cup winning captain – maybe John can emulate him north of the border in the years to come!

WORD SEARCH

```
M I L L E R C B L M M
C A G A L N D Q U N A
L K C E N O U F H I G
E F F K M G F B H C U
I Q D U I N F O R H I
S K O G R E W I G O R
H N N E U C X S E L E
T M A Y T Y N P M L I
L A L P D I A M O N D
B O D D W R U S V R T
X G O T H E N B U R G
```

SCOTT SEVERIN HAS LOST SOME IMPORTANT ABERDEEN WORDS – CAN YOU FIND HELP HIM THESE MISSING WORDS IN THE GRID ABOVE?

DIAMOND
DONALD
DUFF
GOTHENBURG
LANGFIELD

MACKIE
MAGUIRE
MCLEISH
MILLER
NICHOLL

ANSWERS p61

Q&A CHRIS MAGUIRE

What is your favourite ice-cream?
VANILLA OR RASPBERRY RIPPLE

What was your best and worst subject at school?
BEST – PE. WORST – HISTORY

Who did you have a schoolboy crush on?
**BRITNEY SPEARS –
BEFORE SHE CUT HER HAIR OFF!**

If you could buy a ticket for any event in the world, what would it be?
WORLD CUP FINAL

What would your superpower be?
X-RAY VISION

What is your most treasured possession?
MOBILE PHONE

What is your favourite TV programme?
**MATCH OF THE DAY ON A
SATURDAY NIGHT – NEVER MISS IT**

What is the best film ever made?
BRAVEHEART

Who is your favourite cartoon character?
BART SIMPSON

What is your favourite computer game?
PRO EVOLUTION SOCCER

What was the last song/album you downloaded to your iPod?
CHRIS BROWN – FOREVER

Who would play you in the film of your life?
**DON'T REALLY KNOW, BUT McLOVIN
FROM SUPERBAD WOULD BE QUITE FUNNY**

What keeps you awake at night?
NOTHING, UNLESS I HAVE HAD A BAD GAME

What is your favourite item of clothing?
ALWAYS WEAR JEANS

What type/make of football boots do you wear?
ADIDAS PREDATOR (ALWAYS A WHITE PAIR)

What is your greatest achievement in football?
PLAYING IN THE UEFA CUP v BAYERN MUNICH

What is your favourite goal you have scored?
**PROBABLY MY SECOND GOAL AGAINST
FALKIRK WHEN I SCORED FROM THE BY-LINE**

Have you any pre-match rituals?
ALWAYS SPEAK TO MY DAD BEFORE A GAME

When was the last time you used public transport?
TEAM BUS? DOES THAT COUNT?!

Who is your best friend in the dressing room?
ZANDER

Dons Day Out is an ideal way for community groups or birthday boys and girls to raise funds while enjoying a great day out at Pittodrie.

And this season we are pleased to unveil our latetst signing - **Lee Miller** - as the official **Dons Day Out** Ambassador.

For more information on Dons Day Out please visit www.afc.co.uk or call 01224 63 1903

SIMMONS & COMPANY
INTERNATIONAL

QUIZ ANSWERS

p20 CROSSWORD

ACROSS:
1. JIMMY CALDERWOOD
6. ZANDER
10. MAIR
11. LEIGHTON
14. SCOTT
15. RICHARD
17. CONSIDINE

DOWN:
1. JOE HARPER
2. MILLER
3. YOUNG
4. ALEX FERGUSON
5. DEREK
7. ARMY
8. PITTODRIE
9. RED
12. DONS
13. KARIM
14. SMITH
16. DUFF

p58 WORD SEARCH

p26 WHICH WAY?

p42 THE BIG QUIZ

1. FALKIRK
2. LEE MILLER
3. 13
4. JOHN BATEMAN
5. DARREN
6. TEAM RECRUITMENT
7. DUTCH
8. CELTIC
9. IT'S ALLOCATED TO THE RED ARMY
10. 91
11. 1954/55
12. WINNING THE EUROPEAN CUP WINNERS' CUP
13. EUROPEAN CUP WINNERS' CUP AND THE EUROPEAN SUPER CUP
14. SV HAMBURG
15. BAYERN MUNICH
16. KEVIN MCNAUGHTON
17. SEVEN
18. LEAGUE CUP IN 1995/96
19. 55
20. DEAN WINDASS
21. SEVEN
22. EVERTON
23. RAITH ROVERS
24. DUNDEE UNITED
25. JOSH WALKER, DEREK YOUNG, LEE MILLER

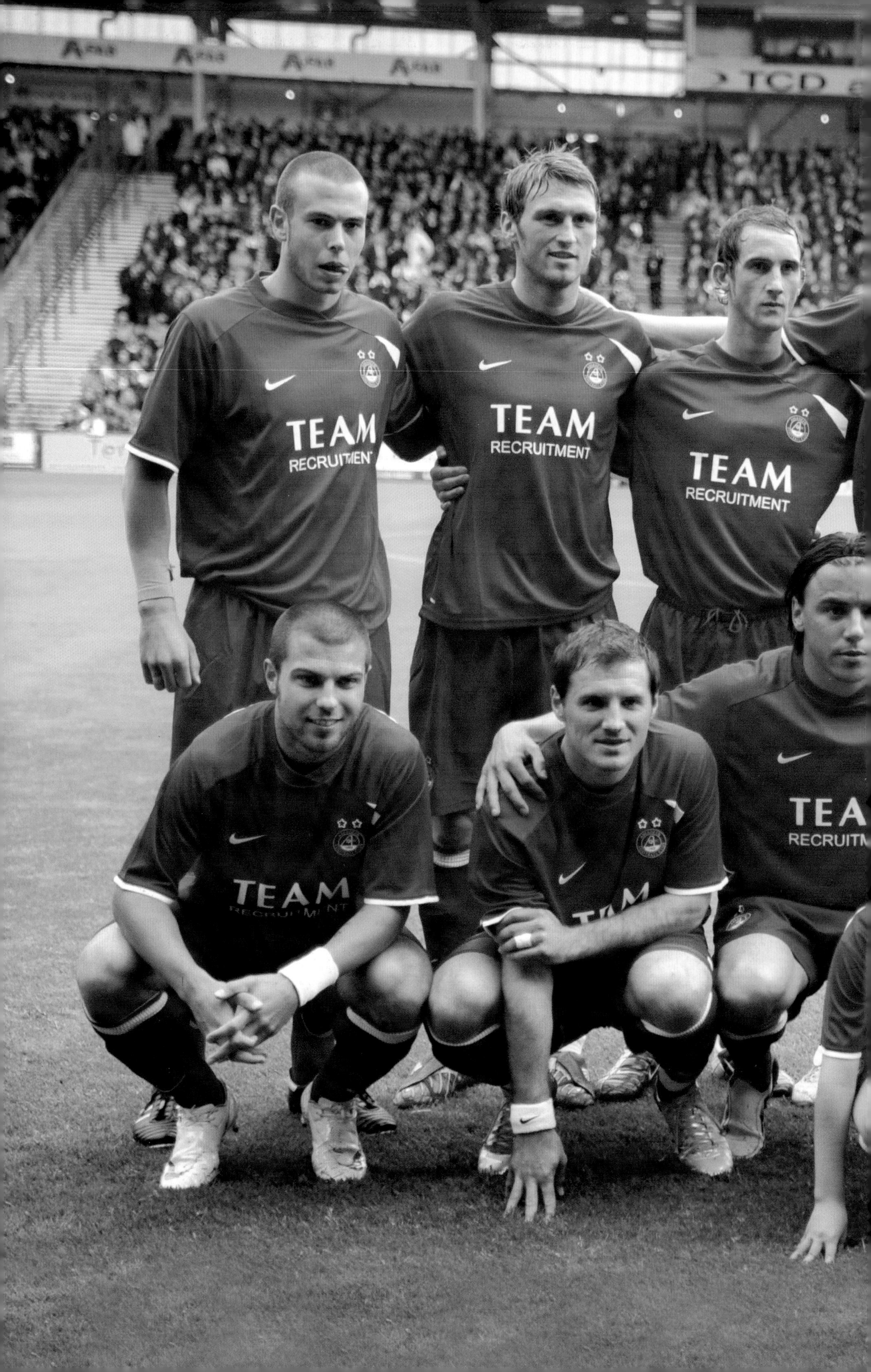
TEAM
RECRUITMENT
TEAM
RECRUITMENT
TEAM
RECRUITMENT
TEAM